Portrait of
SUFFOLK

MARK STAPLES

HALSGROVE

First published in Great Britain in 2010

British Library Cataloguing-in-Publication Data
A CIP record for this title is available from the British Library

ISBN 978 1 84114 993 6

HALSGROVE
Halsgrove House,
Ryelands Industrial Estate,
Bagley Road, Wellington, Somerset TA21 9PZ
Tel: 01823 653777   Fax: 01823 216796
email: sales@halsgrove.com

Part of the Halsgrove group of companies
Information on all Halsgrove titles is available at: www.halsgrove.com

Printed and bound in China by Toppan Leefung Printing Ltd

Dedication

To Shannon and Amy

ACKNOWLEDGEMENTS
Richard Storer, Baylham House Rare Breeds Farm
Patrick Phillips, Kentwell Hall, Long Melford
Lady Xa Tollemache, Helmingham Hall and Gardens
Nikita Hooper, Picture Researcher, the National Trust Photo Library
Peter Cross
Dean Staples

Introduction

Suffolk is a photographer's paradise with its wealth of fine landmarks, monuments and picturesque landscapes. Situated in East Anglia, its varied coastline, beautiful countryside and abundance of towns and villages of historic interest make this a haven for its residents and visitors to the county alike. Hardly surprising then, that Suffolk has been, and still remains, home to some of Britain's most notable people.

Suffolk boasts 40 miles of Heritage Coast, the vast majority of which has been designated an Area of Outstanding Natural Beauty. It is rich in wildlife and offers the possibility of numerous scenic walks. Many of its coastal resorts have a proud fishing tradition and are reminiscent of the 'Great British' coast of yesteryear, having been altered very little by commercialism over time. What better place than Aldeburgh to enjoy fish and chips on the shingle beach, or Southwold, a firm family favourite with its award-winning pier, considered by many as the 'jewel in the crown of the Heritage Coast?' Sadly, much of the eastern coast has fallen victim to the North Sea due to coastal erosion. This is true of Dunwich, once a bustling city, now little more than the size of a village. Legend has it that the bells of its eight churches lost to the sea can still be heard ringing beneath the water at certain tides.

The picturesque Suffolk countryside betrays the county's agricultural heritage, largely arable or mixed. Sugar beet, oilseed rape and winter wheat are amongst the crops grown. The mostly flat landscapes make way for vast skies, which creates a sense of space and the great outdoors.

Suffolk is undeniably rich in history. The county was established from the southern part of the Kingdom of the East Angles, where the Angles settled during the second half of the fifth century. The most important archaeological find of the twentieth century has to be the ancient burial ground of an Anglo-Saxon king at Sutton Hoo in 1939. The ninth century saw the invasion of the Vikings and the death of Edmund, King of the East Angles. Historic Bury St Edmunds became a shrine to St Edmund and from this grew its Benedictine Abbey which now lies in ruins behind its most impressive cathedral, dating from the sixteenth century, with its twenty-first century tower. Many Suffolk villages once enjoyed a thriving wool-trade status, none more so than Lavenham, arguably England's finest medieval town with its abundance of charming half-timber framed buildings. However, Suffolk is not opposed to moving with the times. The Victorian wet docks of Ipswich, Suffolk's county town, have recently undergone a renaissance.

Amongst the most notable people of the county were artists John Constable and Thomas Gainsborough. More recent artists born here are sculptor Elizabeth Frink (1930–1993) responsible for St Edmund's statue in Bury St Edmunds, and Maggi Hambling, whose Scallop sculpture stands on the shingle in Aldeburgh. The Scallop pays homage to Suffolk's most famous composer, Benjamin Britten. Suffolk is also birthplace to actors Ralph Fiennes and Bob Hoskins.

So high in number are Suffolk's curiosities that it is impossible to include them all in one photographic volume. *Portrait of Suffolk* just scratches the surface of what the county has to offer, leaving me with many more places to explore, with my camera in tow.

Mark Staples
www.markstaples.co.uk

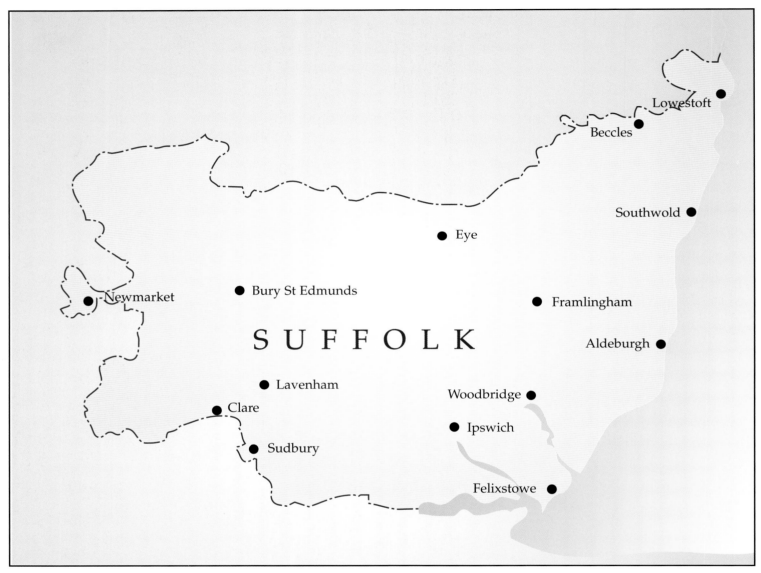

Suffolk and its principle towns.

The Abbey Gate in Bury St Edmunds is a fine example of a fourteenth-century stone gatehouse. It stood as the secular entrance to the Great Courtyard of the former Benedictine Abbey and was used by the servants of the Abbey. The original Abbey Gate was destroyed during the Great Riot of 1327 when the townsfolk revolted against the power that the Abbey held over them.

A lonely tree stands on Benacre Beach. More and more of the East Coast
is regrettably lost to the North Sea year after year.

Left: The coastal town of Aldeburgh was once a significant port and enjoyed a thriving shipbuilding
industry. Sir Francis Drake's *Golden Hind* was constructed here.

Kentwell Hall is a moated Tudor mansion in Long Melford which had stood neglected until 1970, after which it was acquired by Patrick Phillips and family who returned it to its former glory.

The smaller present-day Church of St Andrew was built within the shell of its larger
predecessor. The greater church simply became too much of a burden to maintain
and was thus dismantled and left to ruin by the local people of Covehithe
in the second half of the seventeenth century.

Beach huts immediately spring to mind when one thinks of Southwold, one of the best-known small coastal towns in England. The huts are eagerly sought after and have been known to sell for a small fortune. This quintessential English seaside town is regarded by many as 'the jewel in the crown of the Suffolk Heritage Coast.'

Right: Kersey is famed for its ford or watersplash, branching from the River Brett, and for its Kersey cloth to which the village owes its prosperity.

Baylham House Rare Breeds Farm between Ipswich and Stowmarket describes itself as 'a small livestock farm breeding farm animals that were once common, but are now very rare.' Pictured are two Greyface Dartmoor spring lambs.

Left: Fishing boats rest on the shelved shingle of Aldeburgh beach whilst the fishermen sell the fruits of their early morning catch from wooden huts along the beach.

The original tower of the Church of St Andrew and the newer smaller church can be seen through the arch of the ruin of the older church. It is with regret that one day this church, along with the village of Covehithe, will be consumed by the sea due to coastal erosion.

Right: Early autumn colours on the green in the little village of Hartest.

The Town Pump stands in front of the Shire Hall on Market Hill in the town of Woodbridge. The pump and drinking fountain, erected in 1876, provided water for the livestock market.

Left: Many Suffolk buildings like this Cavendish cottage are still painted in a variant of 'Suffolk pink.' In days gone by, it is assumed that the colour was achieved by mixing natural substances such as pig's blood, red earth or elderberries into the plaster or traditional lime wash.

Pastel-coloured cottages line a side street in Southwold on the Sunrise Coast.

These pretty 'Suffolk Pink' cottages stand between the green and St Mary's Church
at Cavendish and provide this classic picture postcard view.

The hamlet of Felixstowe Ferry is situated at the mouth of the River Deben. Fishing boats bob on the river, and a foot ferry operates between here and the Bawdsey peninsula.

A view that typifies the Suffolk landscape at harvest time. Straw bales lie
in a small field adjacent to St Peter's Church in Freston, near Ipswich.

The town sign casts a shadow on the Ancient House in Clare which sports some of the most impressive pargeting (decorated plasterwork) in Suffolk. In the background stands the Church of St Peter and St Paul.

Kentwell Hall is well-known locally for its recreation of life in Tudor times, and re-enactment of life during the Second World War.

Modern beach huts edge the fine sands of Lowestoft, a popular
seaside resort in the north of the county on the Sunrise Coast.

The boatyard at
Felixstowe Ferry.

Elizabeth Frink's statue of
St Edmund stands adjacent to
St Edmundsbury Cathedral and
reminds us how the historic town of
Bury St Edmunds got its name.
Edmund, King of the East Angles, was
killed by invading Danes in AD869.
In 903, his remains were buried in the
town's monastery, which was later to
become the Abbey, the ruins of which
are located behind the Cathedral.

Right: Stanton Post Mill dates back to
1751 and was relocated to its present
site in 1818. The whole mill, including
sails and all interior machinery, turns
on a single post. The mill has been
fully restored and still produces flour
on a regular basis.

The village sign in Monks Eleigh depicts two monks and one would be forgiven for thinking that a monastery could at one time be found there. This is, however, not so. The monks of Canterbury did actually own the manor, but never lived there.

Situated in the centre of the town, this clock tower is a well-known landmark of Newmarket. It was built by Richard Arber to mark the Golden Jubilee of Queen Victoria, 1887.

The Church of St Peter and St Paul is arguably the most elegant of Suffolk's 'wool churches', so-called as it owes its origins to the wealthy wool merchants of Lavenham, the flourishing centre of England's wool trade during the Middle Ages.

Left: Lobster pots dry in the summer sun on Aldeburgh beach.

Autumn at Needham Lake, a haven for nature and a popular fishing location due to its plentiful stocks of perch, tench, roach, bream, carp and chub.

The House in the Clouds at Thorpeness was once a quirky water tower, but now this folly has been converted to provide unique holiday accommodation.

It is not only Southwold that boasts colourful beach huts. These wooden
structures line the beach of Old Felixstowe.

Right: The pretty Moulton Packhorse Bridge with its four arches crosses
the River Kennett on the old route from Cambridge to Bury St Edmunds.
It is believed to date back to the fifteenth century.

Built between 1165 and 1173 by Henry II, all that remains of Orford Castle today is the Great Tower or Keep. The castle was perhaps once one of the most important in medieval England, due to the role it played in protecting the English coast from the threat of invasion. The ancient town of Orford was a flourishing sea port and fishing village in the Middle Ages. Fishing boats are still very much a feature of the quay.

The Norman Tower in Bury St Edmunds constitutes the belfry of the cathedral next door and was built in the twelth century.

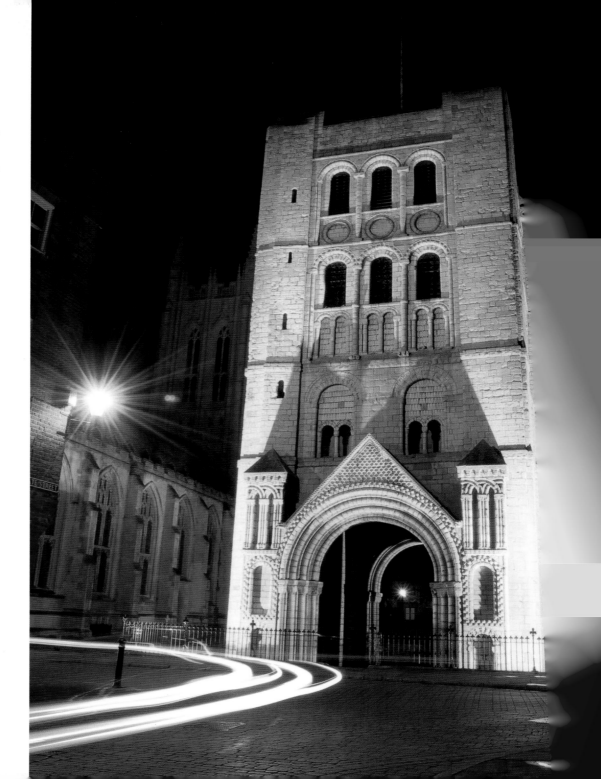

The award-winning Southwold pier stretches 623 feet into the North Sea and is a firm family favourite of holidaymakers. The original pier of the early 1900s was 810 feet in length, but the elements and events of the Second World War reduced the pier at one time to just 60 feet.

Early summer sees poppies spring up on many Suffolk roadsides and occasionally one is treated to a whole field full of these colourful blooms, the seed germinating when the ground has been disturbed by ploughing.

The village of Kersey has no shortage of quaint dwellings for its 300 or so residents.

Located in the centre of the village, Thorpeness 'Meare' is a man-made shallow boating lake with a Peter Pan theme. J M Barrie, author of this fantasy tale, was a family friend of Glencairn Stuart Ogilvie, who created this private mock-tudor seaside resort in the early 1900s out of the former fishing hamlet of Thorpe.

The East Bergholt Church of St Mary the Virgin is of note due to the lack of a spire or tower for its bells. These are instead contained in a bell cage on the north side of the church.

The Mill Hotel in Sudbury sits on the edge of Freemen's Common, where Thomas Gainsborough's father, as a Freeman of Sudbury, grazed his horses.

Pollarded willows showing
fresh spring growth
alongside the Meare
at Thorpeness.

The freshly colour-washed Little Hall stands on the main square in Lavenham.
Once a clothier's house, this fourteenth-century building is now home to
the Suffolk Preservation Society.

Typically Jacobean in style, the almshouses in Thorpeness were actually constructed in the early twentieth century to a design by W G Wilson. The almshouses were viewed by Thorpeness' creator, Glencairn Stuart Ogilvie as the 'handsomest and most imposing buildings in Thorpeness'.

These seafront houses add a splash of colour against the
shingle in the quaint resort of Aldeburgh.

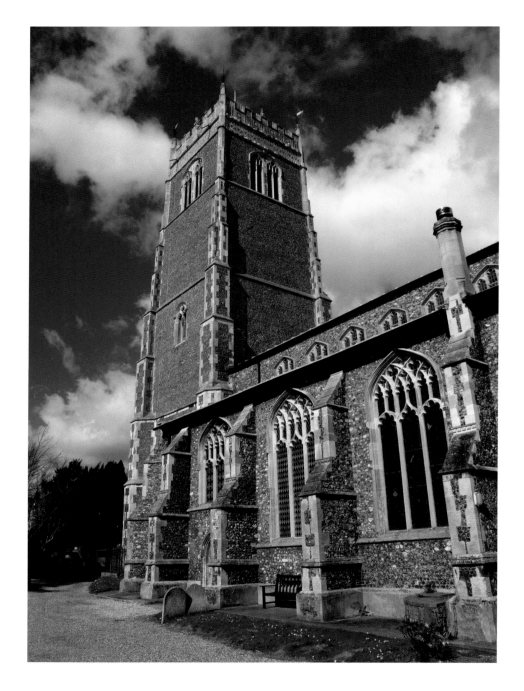

The tower of St Mary's Church in Woodbridge surges over 100 feet into the Suffolk sky.

A carpet of flowering heather covers the ground as far as the eye can see on Dunwich
Heath. This remote stretch of Suffolk Coastline is home to rare wildlife, including the
nightjar, and offers excellent walks and stunning views within this designated
Area of Outstanding Natural Beauty, managed by the National Trust.

The Ferry Boat Inn, Felixstowe Ferry.

Pakenham near Bury St Edmunds claims to be the only village in Britain to have both a
working windmill and a working water mill. The Domesday Survey of 1086 makes
reference to a water mill on the site of the current building.

The doorway to the 'chocolate box' cottage of Cordwainers, Lavenham, 'the most complete medieval town in Britain', boasting over 300 listed buildings.

Right: The vast expanse of shingle beach at Aldeburgh affords plenty of space to get away from it all.

Rain clouds gather over Helmingham Hall, a moated Tudor manor house located in a 400-acre deer park. John Tollemache began its construction in 1480 and it has been in the ownership of the Tollemache family ever since. Although the house is not open to the public, its spectacular gardens open regularly.

Eye Town Hall dates back to 1857. Its clock tower, commissioned to celebrate Queen Victoria's Diamond Jubilee in 1897, was used for locking up local felons. The town's name originates from the Old English for 'island.'

The Old Custom House in Ipswich was constructed in 1845 and lies on the old wet docks.
Once the largest expanse of enclosed water of its sort in England, the docks have enjoyed
an extensive programme of regeneration.

Right: Swans and other waterfowl are an added attraction at the Thorpeness Meare boating lake.

An autumn storm brews over the Thorpeness Meare.

Left: A classic view of Framlingham, a fine example of a late twelfth century English castle, with the Framlingham Mere in the foreground. Framlingham Castle was built between 1189 and 1200 with 13 hollow towers linked by a curtain wall 2.5 metres in depth and 13 metres in height. Only twelve towers remain following the collapse of the thirteenth.

St Edmundsbury Cathedral is the mother church of the diocese of St Edmundsbury and Ipswich, and also the parish church of St James. Although the nave of the present cathedral dates back to 1503, it stands on a much older site of worship, a Norman Abbey having been constructed here in the ninth century.

Right: Suffolk's coastline offers both shingle beaches for long exhilarating walks and golden sandy beaches for youngsters to build their sandcastles.

The post mill which stands next to the House in the Clouds at Thorpeness was originally built at nearby Aldringham in 1803 and was dismantled and moved to its current position in 1922. It is frequently open to the public.

Once moored, a relaxing walk is an enticing proposition along the
Beccles quayside on the River Waveney.

The fourteenth-century Church of St Peter and St Paul, with its flint tower, rises above its neighbouring houses in the small market town of Eye.

Right: The beautiful Abbey Gardens next to the cathedral in Bury St Edmunds offer stunning floral displays, aviaries housing exotic birds, and ducks and waterfowl in the River Lark which runs along the edge of the park.

Maggi Hambling's Scallop stands on the beach between Aldeburgh and Thorpeness and commemorates the life of composer Benjamin Britten who settled in Aldeburgh in 1942 and died there in 1986. The poem by Aldeburgh's George Crabbe about a local fisherman, and Britten's afternoon walks along the beach inspired Britten's opera 'Peter Grimes'. The words 'I hear those voices that will not be drowned,' taken from this opera, are punched into this stainless steel sculpture.

Right: The Southwold lighthouse, established in 1889, towers 31 metres in the midst of a group of Georgian town houses. The lighthouse was automated in 1938.

Left: The River Deben rises near Debenham, passes through Woodbridge pictured here, and becomes a tidal estuary before entering the North Sea at Felixstowe Ferry.

Pakenham on the outskirts of Bury St Edmunds is known as the 'Village of Two Mills'. The Grade II listed tower mill pictured here was built in 1830. The sails still turn thanks to its restoration in 2000, but the mill no longer grinds.

The Old Town Hall of 1868 stands in the bustling centre of Ipswich on Cornhill and nowadays houses a changing line-up of contemporary visual art and designer crafts.

Evening falls on Aldeburgh beach.

Any visitor to Suffolk cannot fail to notice the multitude of colour-washed cottages in many of its picturesque villages, like this house in Kersey.

Right: Stoke-By-Nayland lies on the Suffolk–Essex border in Constable country.

Hawks Mill in Needham Market has now been converted into apartments.

Right: A tender left high and dry by the receding tide on the Orwell at Pin Mill.

The leaning cottage of 'Cordwainers' is a magnificent example of one of the numerous
timber-framed buildings that the medieval town of Lavenham has to offer.
Its archaic name suggests that it was once a shoemaker's home.

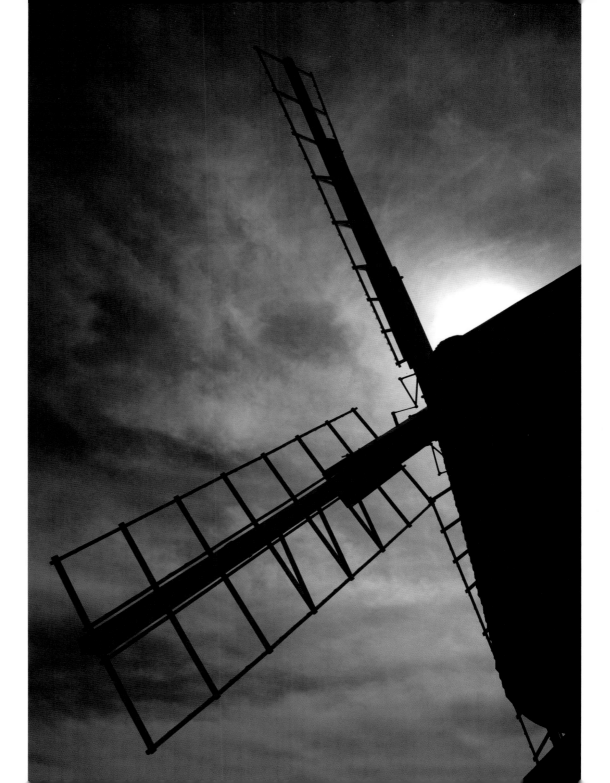

Thorpeness Post Mill
is silhouetted in
the summer sun.

The ruins of one of England's richest Benedictine monasteries lie in
the Abbey Gardens, Bury St Edmunds.

The Guildhall of Corpus Christi in Lavenham dates back to the early sixteenth century and has been described by the National Trust as 'one of the finest timber-framed buildings in Britain.' Today, it houses local history exhibitions and information on the medieval cloth industry of the area.

The Shire Hall in the heart of old Woodbridge on Market Hill was built by Woodbridge's most celebrated resident, Thomas Seckford, a prominent politician, lawyer and official to Queen Elizabeth I.

Right: Autumn sunlight accentuates the fiery autumn colours of these maple leaves.

Pretty cottages edge the village green in Monks Eleigh, some of which date back to the sixteenth century. The Parish Church of St Peter at the top of the green is worthy of a visit.

Left: The late eighteenth century Angel Hotel on Angel Hill in Bury St Edmunds once accommodated Charles Dickens, who chose to feature the hotel in 'Pickwick Papers.'

The remarkable Orwell Bridge was opened in 1982 and took three years to construct.
It takes the A14 across the River Orwell and is 1287 metres in length.

A doorway into the Little Hall in Lavenham pictured in 2006, before its timber framework was painted in coloured lime-wash for preservation purposes.

The *Cygnet* of Harwich pictured on the River Alde in Snape Maltings
is a charming example of a small Thames Barge.

St Mary's Church, in Westley near Bury St Edmunds,
was constructed in 1836 and is reputedly one of
England's oldest concrete churches.

Striking thatched cottages in Somerleyton, better known for
its Tudor-Jacobean mansion, Somerleyton Hall.

It is easy to understand why painter John Constable chose Flatford in the heart of the Dedham Vale as the subject of some of his paintings. An exhibition on the painter is housed in the sixteenth century Bridge Cottage pictured here, just a short distance away from the famous Flatford Mill.

Thatch on the Green, Cockfield, located three and a half miles from Lavenham.

Right: A pub of yesteryear, the Sole Bay Inn at the foot of the lighthouse is the perfect watering hole in Southwold, offering beers and wines from the Adnams Brewery, just a stone's throw away.

From the Victorian wet docks of Ipswich has emerged a contemporary
waterfront of bars, restaurants and residential buildings. The chequered building
of the University Campus Suffolk reflects in the water, disturbed only by a slight
breeze, on this sunny winter's morning

Leiston Abbey, which now lies in ruin, is in the care of English Heritage.
The original Abbey was known as St Mary's Abbey and was founded in Minsmere
in 1182. It was relocated to its current spot in 1363.

The Somerleyton Post Office and Village Store was crowned the winner
of the Community Post Office Award in 2009.

The original Corn Exchange, built in 1503, was obliterated by the Great Fire that swept through the town of Bury St Edmunds in 1608. The present building was constructed in 1861–62 and cost approximately £7000.

A picturesque working corner of the Walled Garden at Helmingham Hall.

A Martello tower, now a water tower, overlooks the bustling Shotley Point Marina.

These Southwold beach huts look out towards the North Sea on this sunny winter's day.

The Angel Hotel in Market Place is reputed to be Lavenham's oldest inn. It was licensed for the first time in 1420 and much of its Tudor character still remains.

A pretty thatched cottage in Polstead. This village is situated on the edge of the Stour Valley and is notorious for the legendary Red Barn Murder when 26-year-old Maria Marten was killed by her lover, William Corder, who was tried and hanged in Bury St Edmunds in 1828. Corder's skeleton was used as a teaching aid at the West Suffolk Hospital, Bury St Edmunds, for many years and is rumoured to have attended socials and dances!

Orford Ness, a wide shingle spit at the mouth of the River Ore, is an important nature reserve managed by the National Trust. During both world wars and the Cold War, secret military tests were undertaken on the Ness by the Ministry of Defence. Pictured here is the Orfordness Lighthouse.

Snape Maltings is renowned for its world class concert hall and for the Aldeburgh Festival. The festival owes its beginnings, in 1948, to composer Benjamin Britten, singer Peter Pears and writer Eric Crozier. Shops, galleries and eateries complete the list of amenities at Snape Maltings, which lies on the River Alde.

Right: The Ipswich Waterfront at night.

The Ramsholt Arms overlooks the River Deben in this unspoilt, tranquil location.

The Tide Mill on the River Deben has become the symbol of Woodbridge and is possibly one of the earliest of its kind in the United Kingdom. It is not known how many mills have stood on this site, but a tide mill was first recorded here in 1170. Clad in traditional white boarding, the current mill is a Grade I listed building.

Comprising little more than coastguard cottages, a row of small houses
and a Martello Tower, Shingle Street is the quintessence of isolation.

Beautiful houses line the main street in the historic village of Debenham which was
mentioned in the Domesday Book and once enjoyed a prosperous wool trade.
The village owes its name to the River Deben upon which it lies.

As its name suggests, the 'Moot' Hall in Aldeburgh was built in 1650 for the purpose of town assemblies and still hosts council meetings today. In 1854, restoration work saw the addition of chimneys based on those of Hampton Court. The town's memorial cross stands in front of the hall.

Left: Walberswick, once a thriving port on the River Blyth, retains many of its unspoilt charms of times gone by. The acres of surrounding marshland and heath have been designated an Area of Outstanding Natural Beauty.

Springtime in the village of Chelsworth, whose main winding road is lined with sixty or so thatched cottages and beautiful houses. The village is easily one of the county's prettiest and is located in the Brett Valley, just 15 miles west of Ipswich.

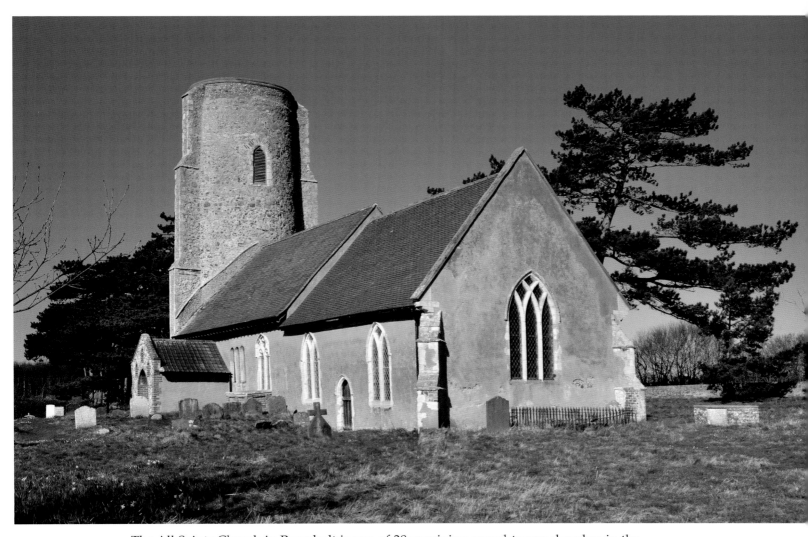

The All Saints Church in Ramsholt is one of 38 surviving round-tower churches in the county. It sits up on a hill and affords beautiful views of the River Deben.

Quintessentially English post boxes outside Woolpit Village Post Office. It is believed that Woolpit takes its name from the archaic 'wulf-pytt,' meaning pit for trapping wolves. The mystery of the Green Children of Woolpit is the village's most fascinating story. In the twelfth century, farmworkers discovered a boy and girl with a green tinge to their skin in a wolf pit in the village. They spoke a strange language and ate only green beans. Local landowner Sir Richard de Calne took them in and, although the boy fell ill and later died, the girl survived, eventually starting to eat normally, learnt English and worked as a servant.

Left: Lowestoft Haven Marina.

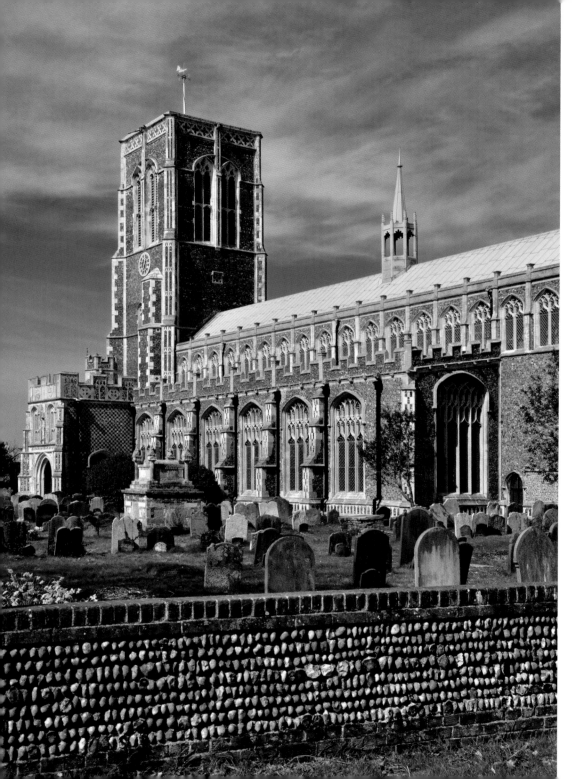

Southwold's Parish Church is dedicated to St Edmund. Construction began in the 1430s to replace a smaller thirteenth-century church that had been destroyed by fire, and lasted approximately 60 years.

The South Lookout, Crag Path, Aldeburgh Beach, has an impressive exterior cast-iron spiral staircase and houses an art and picture framing gallery.

The Town Hall Gardens provide a floral treat and an excellent spot to
watch the world go by on Felixstowe seafront.

Right: The smallest house in Aldeburgh is aptly named 'Fantasia'.

The current cement-rendered building of All Saints Church in Chelsworth is largely fourteenth and fifteenth century, although records mention a church in the village as early as AD926.

What better place than the Butt and Oyster pub to enjoy good food, sample
the finest ale and admire the changing tides of the River Orwell at Pin Mill on
the Shotley Peninsula? The pub's name originates from the oyster fisheries that
were once a significant export from the River Orwell.

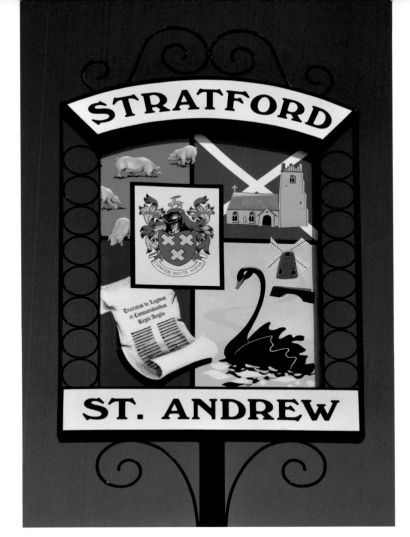

Suffolk ranks second place only to neighbouring Norfolk for the largest number of village signs in England. This colourful example in Stratford St Andrew is one of over 350 signs in the county.

Left: A view along the grass paths between the long flower borders of the Walled Garden towards the moated Helmingham Hall.

Woolpit's village church is dedicated to St Mary and its magnificent spire is visible from some distance around. Like many a Suffolk church, it has evolved from its Norman beginnings. Its double hammer beam roof and abundant angel carvings are worthy of note.

Left: It is not hard to understand why Pin Mill is an artist's haven. Once a popular haunt of smugglers, the hamlet offers charming views and scenic walks along the River Orwell.

Sudbury is birthplace to one of Britain's finest painters, Thomas Gainsborough (1727–1788), famed for both his great landscapes and portraits. This statue stands just yards from the painter's house, in front of St Peter's Church in the town centre.

The East Point Pavillion in Lowestoft, the most easterly town in the United Kingdom.

The inscription under this bronze statue next to the boating lake in Aldeburgh reads: 'This memorial was erected by the people of this borough to Dr 'Robin' P M Acheson who cared for them from 1931 to 1959 and to Dr Nora, his wife, who died 1981 whilst still caring.' Snooks was the Doctor's dog.

Right: Herringfleet Smock Mill lies in the village of the same name on the River Waveney. It was built in the 1820s.

Alliums are a prominent early summer feature of the long borders in Helmingham Hall's beautiful gardens.

Crabbing is a popular pastime in the coastal resort of Walberswick which plays host to the annual British Open Crabbing Championship. Equipped with a single line and bait of one's choice, the winner is the participant who can catch the single heaviest crab within a 90 minute period.

Autumn in the Abbey Gardens, Bury St Edmunds.

A pretty cottage in the village of Ufford, near Woodbridge.

Straw bales in a field in the village of Shotley, about 10 miles south-east of Ipswich. Shotley lies at the tip of a peninsula where the Rivers Stour and Orwell meet at Harwich Harbour.

The village sign in Debenham was erected by villagers to celebrate the Silver Jubilee of Queen Elizabeth II. The sign reflects the historic importance of the wool trade.

Dating back to 1548, the Tudor Christchurch Mansion stands in Christchurch Park in the centre of Ipswich. It has been a free museum since the end of the nineteenth century and its varied collection includes paintings by Gainsborough and Constable.

Left: Oulton Broad offers southern access to the Broads National Park and is an ideal location for sailing and other watersport activities.

Saxtead Green Post Mill was one of many such mills built in Suffolk towards the end of the thirteenth century. The corn mill ceased to operate in 1947, but is still in working order.

Suffolk is blessed with many picture-perfect traditional pubs like this one in the village of Debenham.

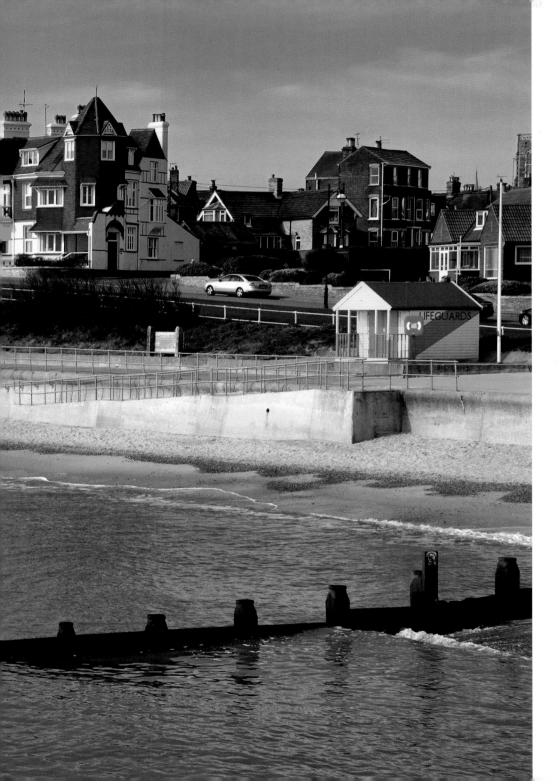

The golden sands of the Southwold beach, viewed here from the pier, are enjoyed whatever the time of the year by local residents and tourists alike.

Some of the country's finest pargeting is to be found on the Ancient House in Ipswich. Images depicting the four discovered continents were worked into the plaster on the building. The Royal Arms of King Charles II were added to the front of the House at a later date.

Right: The Water Clock, built by Tim Hunkin in collaboration with Will Jackson and Jack Trevellian, is one of many amusements on Southwold Pier.

HYPERION
1930 - 1960

Newmarket is the home of British horseracing. The National Museum
of Horseracing is located in the High Street. Nearby, a life-sized
statue stands as a tribute to Hyperion, a thoroughbred
racehorse and exceptional sire.

The Millennium Tower is a recent addition to St Edmundsbury Cathedral, but adds the perfect finishing touch to this fine building. A service to celebrate the completion of the tower was attended by HRH The Prince of Wales and HRH The Duchess of Cornwall on 22 July 2005.

Holy Trinity Church, in the village of Long Melford, is such an extravagant and sizeable 'wool-church' that one would be forgiven for mistaking it for a cathedral. The original church was finished in 1484.